SRA Open Court Reading

Skills Practice

Grade K

MHEonline.com

Copyright © 2016 McGraw-Hill Education

All rights reserved. No part of this publication may be reproduced or distributed in any form or by any means, or stored in a database or retrieval system, without the prior written consent of McGraw-Hill Education, including, but not limited to, network storage or transmission, or broadcast for distance learning.

Send all inquiries to:
McGraw-Hill Education
8787 Orion Place
Columbus, OH 43240

McGraw Hill Education

MHEonline.com

Copyright © 2016 McGraw-Hill Education

All rights reserved. No part of this publication may be
reproduced or distributed in any form or by any means,
or stored in a database or retrieval system, without the
prior written consent of McGraw-Hill Education,
including, but not limited to, network storage or
transmission, or broadcast for distance learning.

Send all inquiries to:
McGraw-Hill Education
8787 Orion Place
Columbus, OH 43240

ISBN: 978-0-07-669188-3
MHID: 0-07-669188-8

Printed in the United States of America.

4 5 6 7 8 9 LOV 21 20 19 18 17

Table of Contents

Copyright © McGraw-Hill Education

Unit 3

Unit 4

Copyright © McGraw-Hill Education

Unit 5

Unit 6

Copyright © McGraw-Hill Education

Name _____ **Date** _____

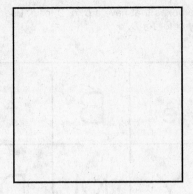

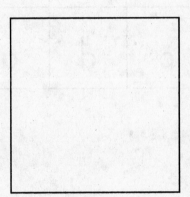

Copyright © McGraw-Hill Education

Directions: Draw a smiley face in each box just like the one pictured.

Skills Practice 1 • Penmanship

Name _____ **Date** _____

Directions: Color the boxes that have a *C, c, D,* or *d.* Use one color
for *C, c,* and another color for *D, d.*

e	B	t	c	B	R
Y	M	D	H	b	C
B	b	E	C	M	d
c	d	a	F	D	g

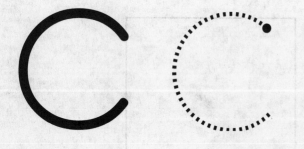 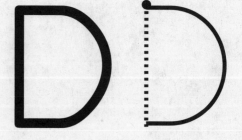

Directions: Start at the large dot and follow the dotted line to
complete each letter.

Copyright © McGraw-Hill Education

Alphabetic Knowledge • *Skills Practice 1*

E E D D

B B F F

H H K K

T T L L

Directions: Practice making lines. Start at the large dot and follow
the dotted line to complete each letter.

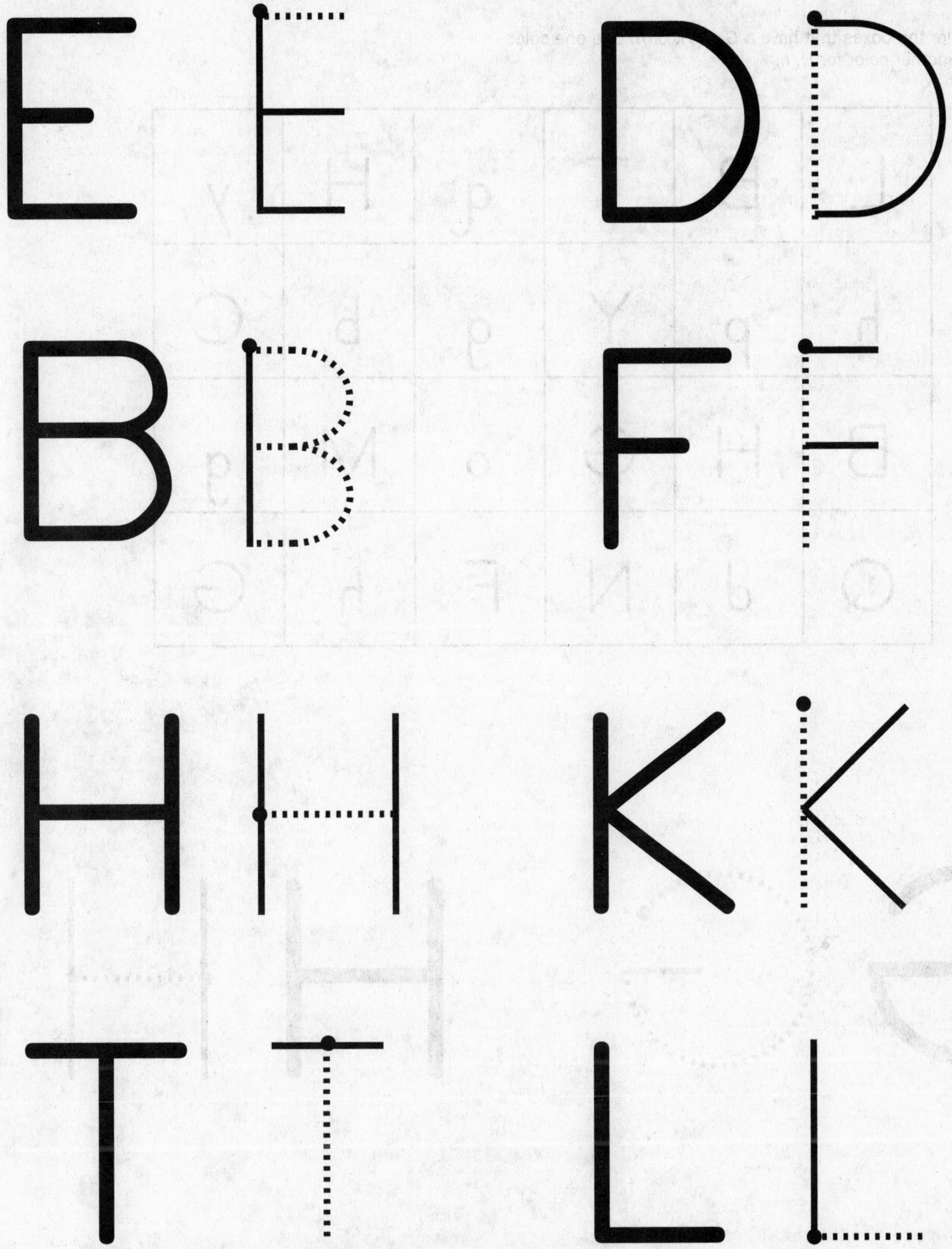

Copyright © McGraw-Hill Education

Skills Practice 1 • Penmanship

Directions: Color the boxes that have a G, g, H, or h. Use one color
for G, g, and another color for H, h.

L	B	T	q	H	y
h	p	Y	g	b	C
B	H	G	o	M	g
Q	d	N	F	h	G

G G   H H

Directions: Start at the large dot and follow the dotted line to
complete each letter.

Copyright © McGraw-Hill Education

Directions: Find and circle capital letters A, B, C, D, E, F, G, and H.

Copyright © McGraw-Hill Education

Skills Practice 1 • Alphabetic Knowledge

Directions: Find and circle lowercase letters a, b, c, d, e, f, g, and h.

Alphabetic Knowledge • *Skills Practice 1*

Copyright © McGraw-Hill Education

1.    Anne   anne

2.    adam   Adam

3.    Dan   dan

4.    carol   Carol

Copyright © McGraw-Hill Education

Directions: Circle the name that is written correctly with a capital letter.

E E

Z Z

A A

F F

H H

G G

T T

L L

Directions: Practice making lines. Start at the large dot and follow
the dotted line to complete each letter.

Copyright © McGraw-Hill Education

Directions: Color the boxes that have a *K, k, L,* or *l.* Use one color
for *K, k,* and another color for *L, l.*

L	K	t	q	H	I
h	i	Y	L	b	C
k	H	l	o	K	I
Q	d	N	F	h	k

Copyright © McGraw-Hill Education

K K   L L

Directions: Start at the large dot and follow the dotted line to
complete each letter.

Skills Practice 1 • Alphabetic Knowledge

E	M	a	B	h	n
Y	v	n	t	M	R
f	N	C	m	g	A
M	T	s	G	e	m
b	m	H	c	N	F
S	V	r	M	y	n

Directions: Color the boxes that have an *M*, *m*, *N*, or *n*. Use one color for *M*, *m*, and another color for *N*, *n*.

Copyright © McGraw-Hill Education

 O   p

 p   O

 b   r

 R   b

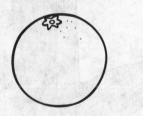 o   P

 B   R

Copyright © McGraw-Hill Education

Directions: Find and circle letters *O*, *o*, *P*, and *p*.

Skills Practice 1 • Alphabetic Knowledge   UNIT 1 • Lesson 2 • Day 4   **11**

Name _____ Date _____

Directions: Connect the dots, in order from A–P, to complete the picture of the bluebird.

Alphabetic Knowledge • *Skills Practice 1*

Copyright © McGraw-Hill Education

Name _____ **Date** _____

A A W W

V V K K

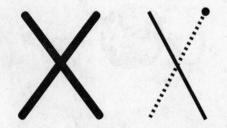

X X M M

Copyright © McGraw-Hill Education

Directions: Start at the large dot and follow the dotted line to complete each letter.

Name _____ Date _____

1.

2.

3.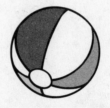

4.

5.

Copyright © McGraw-Hill Education

Directions: Draw a circle around the noun that names the thing in each row.

A A N N

V V W W

X X M M

Directions: Start at the large dot and follow the dotted line to complete each letter.

Copyright © McGraw-Hill Education

 S

 U

 t

 s

 f

 W

 u

 T

 I

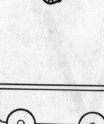

Copyright © McGraw-Hill Education

Directions: Find and circle letters *S, s, T, t, U,* and *u*.

Alphabetic Knowledge • *Skills Practice 1*

A A N N

V V W W

X X M M

Directions: Start at the large dot and follow the dotted line to
complete each letter.

Copyright © McGraw-Hill Education

Directions: Color the boxes that have an X, x, Y, y, Z, or z. Use
three different colors: one for X, x, one for Y, y, and one for Z, z.

Y	K	t	q	H	Z
H	Z	y	X	b	s
k	H	S	z	K	Y
x	d	z	F	h	k

Copyright © McGraw-Hill Education

Directions: Start at the large dot and follow the dotted line to
complete each letter.

Directions: Connect the dots in alphabetical order from *N* to *Z* to complete the picture of the willow tree.

Copyright © McGraw-Hill Education

Skills Practice 1 • Alphabetic Knowledge

1. dog

2. ball

3. teacher

4. wagon

5. castle

Copyright © McGraw-Hill Education

Directions: Circle the picture that matches the word I say.

D D   O O

B B   R R

P P   Q Q

p p   b b

Directions: Start at the large dot and follow the dotted line to complete each letter.

Copyright © McGraw-Hill Education

C C   Q Q

G G   d d

O O   p p

e e   g

Copyright © McGraw-Hill Education

Directions: Start at the large dot and follow the dotted line to complete each letter.

D D B B

O O R R

Q Q G G

 p e

Copyright © McGraw-Hill Education

Directions: Start at the large dot and follow the dotted line to
complete each letter.

1.

2.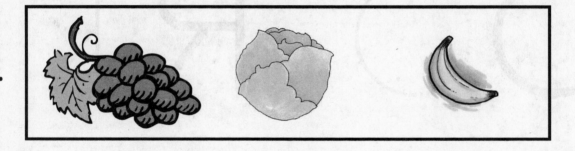

3.

4.

Directions: Circle the picture in each row that matches what I say.

Copyright © McGraw-Hill Education

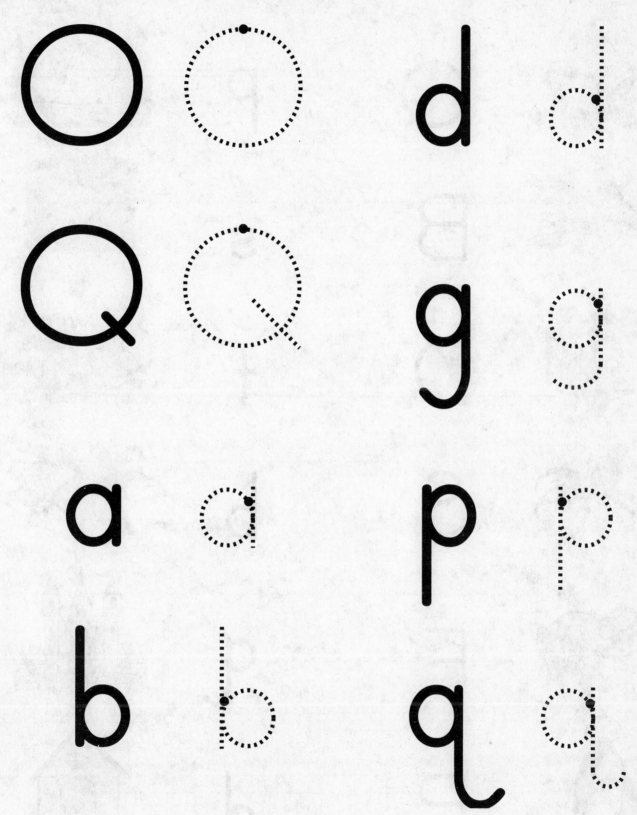

Copyright © McGraw-Hill Education

Directions: Start at the large dot and follow the dotted line to
complete each letter.

 Q

 p

 B

 s

 D

 f

 S

 b

 F

 q

 P

 d

Directions: Draw a line from the capital letter to its matching lowercase letter.

Alphabetic Knowledge • *Skills Practice 1*

Copyright © McGraw-Hill Education

g g   d d

a a    O O

Q Q   q q

p p   b b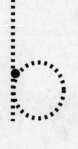

Copyright © McGraw-Hill Education

Directions: Start at the large dot and follow the dotted line to complete each letter.

Copyright © McGraw-Hill Education

Directions: Look at the number on the monkeys' shirts. Draw the correct number of circles inside each basket.

Copyright © McGraw-Hill Education

Name _____ **Date** _____

1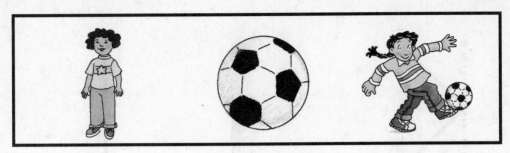

2.

3.

4.

5.

Directions: Circle the picture that shows an action.

K K L L

A A F F

T T D D

B B P P

Directions: Start at the large dot and follow the dotted line to
complete each letter.

Penmanship • *Skills Practice 1*

Copyright © McGraw-Hill Education

Tt	Nn	Ee	Ss

tens	sent
spin	mint
nets	pens
rest	nest

Copyright © McGraw-Hill Education

Directions: Circle the words that contain all the letters listed at the top of the page.

A A   K K

V V   X X

M M   W W

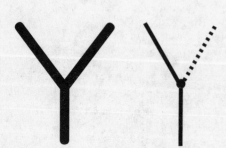 Y Y   N

Copyright © McGraw-Hill Education

Directions: Start at the large dot and follow the dotted line to complete each letter.

Name _____ **Date** _____

G G   B B

D D   C C

Q Q   g g

p p   b b

Directions: Start at the large dot and follow the dotted line to complete each letter.

Copyright © McGraw-Hill Education

Skills Practice 1 • Penmanship

Copyright © McGraw-Hill Education

Name _____ **Date** _____

1. house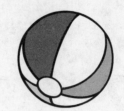

2. toy

3. sat

4. three

5. sing

6. jog

Directions: I will say the word in each row. Circle the picture of
the object that has a rhyming name.

S s

S

s

_____   _____

_____   _____

Copyright © McGraw-Hill Education

Directions: Write the capital and lowercase forms of the letter Ss.
Write the letter s under the picture whose name begins with the /s/ sound.

Ss

_____

- - - - - - - - - - - - - - -

_____

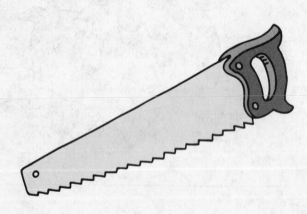

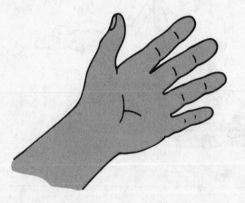

_____

- - - - - - - - - - - - - - -

_____

Directions: Write the letter s under each picture whose name begins with the /s/ sound.

Alphabetic Principle • *Skills Practice 1*

Copyright © McGraw-Hill Education

_____

- - - - - - - - - - - - - - - -

_____

_____

- - - - - - - - - - - - - - - -

_____

_____

- - - - - - - - - - - - - - - -

_____

_____

- - - - - - - - - - - - - - - -

_____

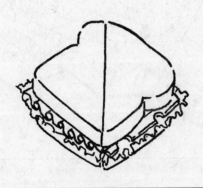

_____

- - - - - - - - - - - - - - - -

_____

_____

- - - - - - - - - - - - - - - -

_____

Copyright © McGraw-Hill Education

Directions: Write the letter s under each picture whose name ends with the /s/ sound.

Mm

M _ _ _ _ _ _ _ _ _ _ _ _ _ _ _ _ _ _

m _ _ _ _ _ _ _ _ _ _ _ _ _ _ _ _ _ _

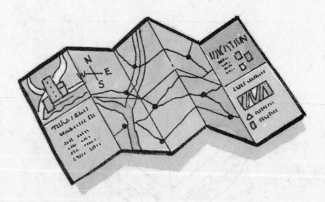

_____

- - - - - - - - - - - - - - - - - - -

_____

_____

- - - - - - - - - - - - - - - - - - -

_____

Directions: Write the capital and lowercase forms of the letter *Mm*. Write the letter *m* under the picture whose name begins with the /m/ sound.

Copyright © McGraw-Hill Education

_____

- - - - - - - - - - - - - - - -

_____

_____

- - - - - - - - - - - - - - - -

_____

Copyright © McGraw-Hill Education

_____

- - - - - - - - - - - - - - - -

_____

_____

- - - - - - - - - - - - - - - -

_____

Directions: Write the letter _m_ under each picture whose name begins with the /m/ sound.

Name _____ **Date** _____

_____

- - - - - - - - - - - - - - - - - - -

_____

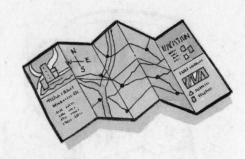

_____

- - - - - - - - - - - - - - - - - - -

_____

_____

- - - - - - - - - - - - - - - - - - -

_____

_____

- - - - - - - - - - - - - - - - - - -

_____

_____

- - - - - - - - - - - - - - - - - - -

_____

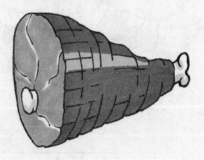

_____

- - - - - - - - - - - - - - - - - - -

_____

Copyright © McGraw-Hill Education

Directions: Write the capital letter *M* under each picture whose name begins with the /m/ sound.
Write the lowercase letter *m* under each picture whose name ends with the /m/ sound.

Alphabetic Principle • *Skills Practice 1*

_____   _____

- - - - - - - - - - - - - - - - -   - - - - - - - - - - - - - - - - -

_____   _____

_____   _____

- - - - - - - - - - - - - - - - -   - - - - - - - - - - - - - - - - -

_____   _____

Copyright © McGraw-Hill Education

Directions: Write the letter *m* under the picture if it begins with the /m/ sound. Write the letter s
under the picture if it begins with the /s/ sound.

_____

- - - - - - - - - - - - - - - - - -

_____

_____

- - - - - - - - - - - - - - - - - -

_____

_____

- - - - - - - - - - - - - - - - - -

_____

_____

- - - - - - - - - - - - - - - - - -

_____

Copyright © McGraw-Hill Education

Directions: Write the letter *m* under the picture if it begins with the /m/ sound. Write the letter *s* under the picture if it begins with the /s/ sound.

1. I like dogs.
    Ilikedogs.

2. We play games.
    Weplaygames.

3. Mycarisred.
    My car is red.

4. She walks with me.
    Shewalkswithme.

Copyright © McGraw-Hill Education

Directions: Circle the sentence that is written correctly.

Dd

D _____

d _____

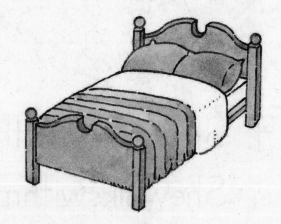

_____   _____

Directions: Write the capital and lowercase forms of the letter *Dd*.
Write the letter *d* under the picture whose name begins with the /d/ sound.

Copyright © McGraw-Hill Education

_____

_ _ _ _ _ _ _ _ _ _ _ _ _

_____

_____

_ _ _ _ _ _ _ _ _ _ _ _ _

_____

Copyright © McGraw-Hill Education

Directions: Write the letter *d* under each picture whose name begins with the /d/ sound.

be

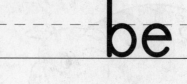

han

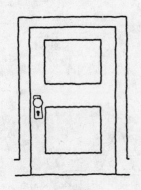

oor

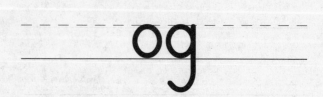

og

Copyright © McGraw-Hill Education

Directions: Listen as I say each picture name. Write a *d* to complete each word.

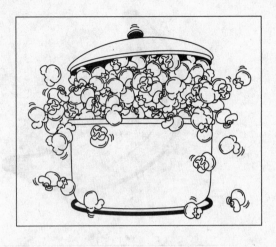

P ------------------------------------

p ------------------------------------

_____   _____

- - - - - - - - - - -   - - - - - - - - - - -

_____   _____

Directions: Write the capital and lowercase forms of the letter *Pp*. Write the letter *p* under the picture whose name begins with the /p/ sound.

Copyright © McGraw-Hill Education

_____

- - - - - - - - - - - - - - - - -

_____

_____

- - - - - - - - - - - - - - - - -

_____

Copyright © McGraw-Hill Education

Directions: Write the letter *p* under each picture whose name begins with the /p/ sound.

_____

- - - - - - - - - - - - - - - -

_____

_____

- - - - - - - - - - - - - - - -

_____

_____

- - - - - - - - - - - - - - - -

_____

_____

- - - - - - - - - - - - - - - -

_____

_____

- - - - - - - - - - - - - - - -

_____

_____

- - - - - - - - - - - - - - - -

_____

Copyright © McGraw-Hill Education

Directions: Write the letter *p* under each picture whose name ends with the /p/ sound.

ail

aint

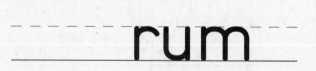
rum

Copyright © McGraw-Hill Education

Directions: Listen as I say each picture name. Write a *d* or *p* to complete each word.

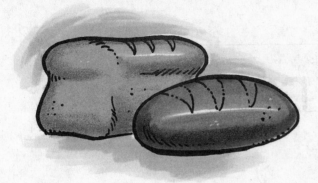

brea

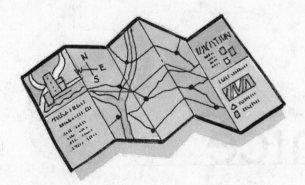

ma

be

Copyright © McGraw-Hill Education

Directions: Listen as I say each picture name. Write a *d* or *p* to complete each word.

1. The dog ran

2. Apples are red

3. You are nice

4. My bike is red

Directions: Trace the capital letter that begins each sentence and add a period at the end of each sentence.

Copyright © McGraw-Hill Education

A ----------------------------------

a ----------------------------------

_____   _____
- - - - - - - - - - -   - - - - - - - - - - -
_____   _____

Directions: Write the capital and lowercase forms of the letter *Aa*. Write the letter *a* under the picture whose name has the /a/ sound.

Copyright © McGraw-Hill Education

_____

- - - - - - - - - - - - - - - - -

_____

_____

- - - - - - - - - - - - - - - - -

_____

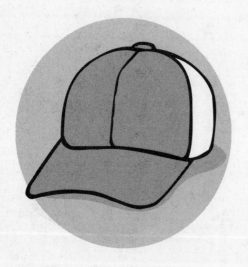

_____

- - - - - - - - - - - - - - - - -

_____

_____

- - - - - - - - - - - - - - - - -

_____

Directions: Write the letter *a* under each picture whose name has the /a/ sound.

Alphabetic Principle • *Skills Practice 1*

Copyright © McGraw-Hill Education

Name _____ **Date** _____

bat

_____

- - - - - - - - - - - - -

_____

bag

_____

- - - - - - - - - - - - -

_____

man

_____

- - - - - - - - - - - - -

_____

pan

_____

- - - - - - - - - - - - -

_____

Copyright © McGraw-Hill Education

Directions: Listen as I say each picture name. Write s, m, or a if the word has the /s/, /m/, or /a/ sound.

Name _____ **Date** _____

can

_____
- - - - - - - - - - - - -
_____

sun

_____
- - - - - - - - - - - - -
_____

mug

_____
- - - - - - - - - - - - -
_____

hat

_____
- - - - - - - - - - - - -
_____

Copyright © McGraw-Hill Education

Directions: Listen as I say each picture name. Write s, m, or a if the word has the /s/, /m/, or /a/ sound.

Penmanship • *Skills Practice 1*

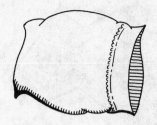

Copyright © McGraw-Hill Education

Directions: Draw a line between the two pictures whose names begin with the /d/ sound. Draw a line between the two pictures whose names begin with the /p/ sound. Draw a line between the two pictures whose names begin with the /a/ sound.

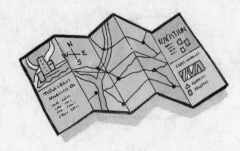

_____
- - - - - - - - - - - - - - - - - - - -
_____

_____
- - - - - - - - - - - - - - - - - - - -
_____

_____
- - - - - - - - - - - - - - - - - - - -
_____

_____
- - - - - - - - - - - - - - - - - - - -
_____

_____
- - - - - - - - - - - - - - - - - - - -
_____

_____
- - - - - - - - - - - - - - - - - - - -
_____

Directions: Listen as I say each picture name. Write the letter that begins each word. Write an *a* next to the other letter if the word has the /a/ sound.

Penmanship • *Skills Practice 1*

Copyright © McGraw-Hill Education

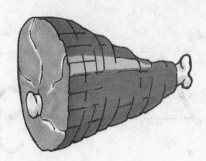

_____

- - - - - - - - - - - -

_____

_____

- - - - - - - - - - - -

_____

_____

- - - - - - - - - - - -

_____

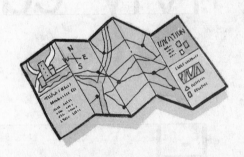

_____

- - - - - - - - - - - -

_____

_____

- - - - - - - - - - - -

_____

Copyright © McGraw-Hill Education

Directions: Listen as I say each picture name. Write the letter that ends each word.

1. A dog barks

2. My cat jumps

3. Horses run fast

4. You can read

Directions: Trace the capital letter that begins each sentence and add a period at the end of each sentence.

Copyright © McGraw-Hill Education

Name _____ **Date** _____

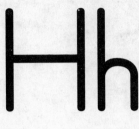

Hh

H ─ ─ ─ ─ ─ ─ ─ ─ ─ ─ ─ ─ ─ ─ ─ ─

h ─ ─ ─ ─ ─ ─ ─ ─ ─ ─ ─ ─ ─ ─ ─ ─

Copyright © McGraw-Hill Education

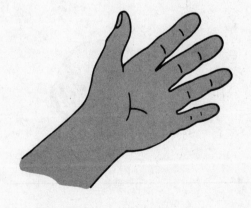

_____   _____
─ ─ ─ ─ ─ ─ ─ ─ ─ ─ ─   ─ ─ ─ ─ ─ ─ ─ ─ ─ ─ ─
_____   _____

Directions: Write the capital and lowercase forms of the letter *Hh*. Write the letter *h* under the picture whose name begins with the /h/ sound.

_____

- - - - - - - - - - - - -

_____

_____

- - - - - - - - - - - - -

_____

Copyright © McGraw-Hill Education

Directions: Write the letter *h* under each picture whose name begins with the /h/ sound.

Alphabetic Principle • *Skills Practice 1*

Name _____ **Date** _____

 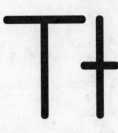

Copyright © McGraw-Hill Education

Directions: Write the capital and lowercase forms of the letter *Tt*. Write the letter *t* under the picture whose name begins with the /t/ sound.

_____

- - - - - - - - - - - - - - -

_____

Copyright © McGraw-Hill Education

_____

- - - - - - - - - - - - - - -

_____

Directions: Write the letter *t* under each picture whose name begins with the /t/ sound.

Penmanship • *Skills Practice 1*

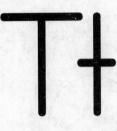

T

t

_____

_ _ _ _ _ _ _ _ _ _ _ _

_____

_ _ _ _ _ _ _ _ _ _ _ _

Copyright © McGraw-Hill Education

Directions: Write the capital and lowercase forms of the letter *Tt*.
Write the letter *t* under the picture whose name ends with the /t/ sound.

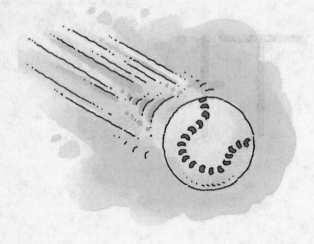

_____

- -

_____

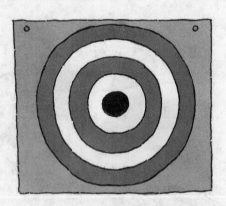

_____

- -

_____

Copyright © McGraw-Hill Education

Directions: Write the letter *t* under each picture whose name ends
with the /t/ sound.

Name _____ **Date** _____

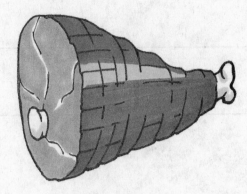

_____
- - - - - - - - - - - - - -
a m
_____

_____
- - - - - - - - - - - - - -
o p
_____

_____
- - - - - - - - - - - - - -
a t
_____

Copyright © McGraw-Hill Education

Directions: Listen as I say each picture name. Write an *h* or a *t* to complete each word.

Skills Practice 1 • Penmanship

UNIT 4 • Lesson 1 • Day 5 **67**

_____

ug

_____

10

_____

en

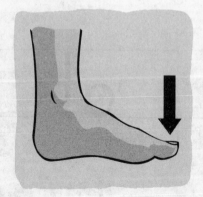

_____

oe

Directions: Listen as I say each picture name. Write an *h* or a *t* to complete each word.

Penmanship • *Skills Practice 1*

Copyright © McGraw-Hill Education

1. Do you like to paint?
   I like to read.

2. Here is my lunchbox.
   Do you like to swim?

3. Is it raining?
   Tara knows how to swim.

4. Where is your sock?
   The pen is blue.

5. This is my mom's car.
   Do you ride the school bus?

Copyright © McGraw-Hill Education

Directions: Listen as I read each sentence. Circle the sentence that asks a question.

Nn

N

n

Directions: Write the capital and lowercase forms of the letter *Nn*.
Write the letter *n* under the picture whose name begins with the
/n/ sound.

Copyright © McGraw-Hill Education

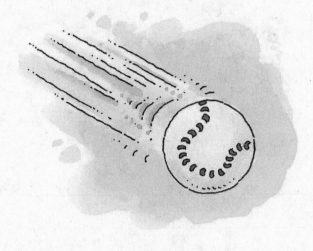

_____

- - - - - - - - - - - - - - - - -

_____

Copyright © McGraw-Hill Education

_____

- - - - - - - - - - - - - - - - -

_____

Directions: Write the letter *n* under each picture whose name begins with the /n/ sound.

_____

- - - - - - - - - - - - - - -

_____

_____

- - - - - - - - - - - - - - -

_____

_____

- - - - - - - - - - - - - - -

_____

_____

- - - - - - - - - - - - - - -

_____

_____

- - - - - - - - - - - - - - -

_____

_____

- - - - - - - - - - - - - - -

_____

Directions: Write the letter *n* under each picture whose name ends with the /n/ sound.

Alphabetic Principle • *Skills Practice 1*

Copyright © McGraw-Hill Education

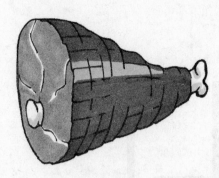

_____

- - - - - - - - - - - - - - - - - -

_____

_____

- - - - - - - - - - - - - - - - - -

_____

_____

- - - - - - - - - - - - - - - - - -

_____

_____

- - - - - - - - - - - - - - - - - -

_____

_____

- - - - - - - - - - - - - - - - - -

_____

_____

- - - - - - - - - - - - - - - - - -

_____

Directions: Write the letter n under each picture whose name ends with the /n/ sound.

Copyright © McGraw-Hill Education

Skills Practice 1 • Alphabetic Principle

L l

L -

l -

_____   _____

- - - - - - - - - -   - - - - - - - - - -

Copyright © McGraw-Hill Education

Directions: Write the capital and lowercase forms of the letter *Ll*. Write the letter *l* under the picture whose name begins with the /l/ sound.

_____
- - - - - - - - - - - - - - - - -
_____

_____
- - - - - - - - - - - - - - - - -
_____

Copyright © McGraw-Hill Education

_____
- - - - - - - - - - - - - - - - -
_____

_____
- - - - - - - - - - - - - - - - -
_____

Directions: Write the letter *l* under each picture whose name begins with the /l/ sound.

Copyright © McGraw-Hill Education

Directions: Draw a circle around each object in the picture whose name ends with the /l/ sound. Write the capital form of the letter *Ll*.

Copyright © McGraw-Hill Education

Directions: Draw a circle around each object in the picture whose name ends with the /l/ sound. Write the lowercase form of the letter Ll.

ails

et

ock

Copyright © McGraw-Hill Education

Directions: Listen as I say each picture name. Write an *n* or an *l* to complete each word.

Copyright © McGraw-Hill Education

Name _____   **Date** _____

pai

10

te

fa

Directions: Listen as I say each picture name. Write an *n* or an *l* to complete each word.

1. The boy was hungry . ?

2. Who is it . ?

3. I cleaned my room . ?

4. The cat ran up the tree . ?

5. Are you the teacher . ?

6. Was the boy hungry . ?

Copyright © McGraw-Hill Education

Directions: Listen carefully as I read each sentence. Circle the correct end mark.

nch

nsect

nfant

Copyright © McGraw-Hill Education

Directions: Listen as I say each picture name. Write the missing letter *i* to complete each word.

Name _____ **Date** _____

Date _____

_____

- - - - - - - - - - - - - -

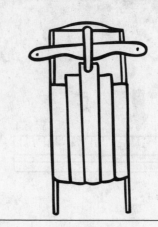

_____

- - - - - - - - - - - - - -

_____

- - - - - - - - - - - - - -

_____

_____

- - - - - - - - - - - - - -

_____

_____

- - - - - - - - - - - - - -

_____

_____

- - - - - - - - - - - - - -

_____

Copyright © McGraw-Hill Education

Directions: Listen carefully as I name each picture. Write the letter *i* under the picture if you hear the /i/ sound.

Alphabetic Principle • *Skills Practice 1*

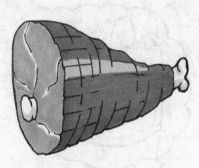

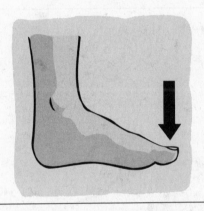

Copyright © McGraw-Hill Education

Directions: Listen carefully as I name each picture. Write *h* or *t* under each picture whose name begins with the /h/ or /t/ sound. Write *i* beside the other letter if you hear the /i/ sound.

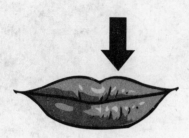

_____

- - - - - - - - - - -

_____

_____

- - - - - - - - - - -

_____

_____

- - - - - - - - - - -

_____

_____

- - - - - - - - - - -

_____

_____

- - - - - - - - - - -

_____

_____

- - - - - - - - - - -

_____

Directions: Listen carefully as I name each picture. Write the letter *n* under the pictures whose names begin with the /n/ sound. Write the letter *l* under the pictures whose names begin with the /l/ sound. Write *i* beside the other letter if you hear the /i/ sound.

84 UNIT 4 • Lesson 3 • Day 4

Alphabetic Principle • *Skills Practice 1*

Copyright © McGraw-Hill Education

Copyright © McGraw-Hill Education

Directions: Listen carefully as I name each picture. Write *h*, *t*, *n*, or *l* under each picture whose name begins with the /h/, /t/, /n/, or /l/ sound. Write i beside the other letter if you hear the /i/ sound.

_____

- - - - - - - - - - - - - - -

_____

_____

- - - - - - - - - - - - - - -

_____

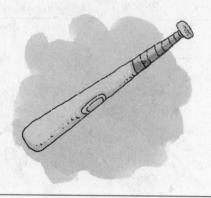

_____

- - - - - - - - - - - - - - -

_____

_____

- - - - - - - - - - - - - - -

_____

_____

- - - - - - - - - - - - - - -

_____

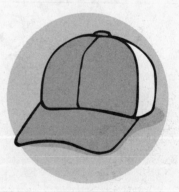

_____

- - - - - - - - - - - - - - -

_____

Copyright © McGraw-Hill Education

Directions: Listen carefully as I name each picture. Write *t*, *n*, or *l* under each picture whose name ends with the /t/, /n/, or /l/ sound. Write *i* beside the other letter if you hear the /i/ sound.

1. Do you have a dog?
Do you have a dog with
spots?

2. Does he want to play?
Does he want to
play baseball?

3. Where is your kite?
Where is your striped
kite?

4. When do they like to eat?
When do they like to eat
dinner?

Copyright © McGraw-Hill Education

Directions: Listen as I read each pair of sentences. Circle the sentence that gives the most detail.

Bb

B _

b _

_____

_____

Directions: Write the capital and lowercase forms of the letter *Bb*. Write the letter *b* under the picture whose name begins with the /b/ sound.

Copyright © McGraw-Hill Education

_____

- - - - - - - - - - - - - -

_____

_____

- - - - - - - - - - - - - -

_____

_____

- - - - - - - - - - - - - -

_____

_____

- - - - - - - - - - - - - -

_____

Copyright © McGraw-Hill Education

Directions: Write the letter *b* under each picture whose name begins with the /b/ sound.

_____

- - - - - - - - - - - - - - - - - - - -

_____

_____

- - - - - - - - - - - - - - - - - - - -

_____

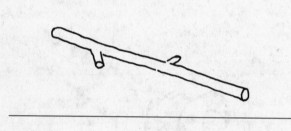

_____

- - - - - - - - - - - - - - - - - - - -

_____

_____

- - - - - - - - - - - - - - - - - - - -

_____

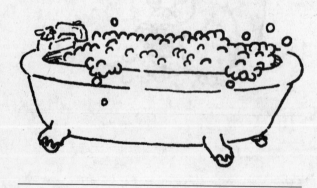

_____

- - - - - - - - - - - - - - - - - - - -

_____

_____

- - - - - - - - - - - - - - - - - - - -

_____

Copyright © McGraw-Hill Education

Directions: Write the letter *b* under each picture whose name ends with the /b/ sound.

Name _____ **Date** _____

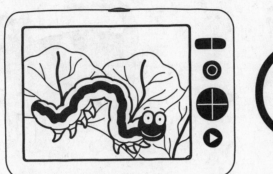

Cc

C

c

Directions: Write the capital and lowercase forms of the letter Cc. Write the letter c under the picture whose name begins with the /k/ sound.

Copyright © McGraw-Hill Education

Skills Practice 1 • Penmanship

Directions: Write the letter c under each picture whose name begins with the /k/ sound.

Copyright © McGraw-Hill Education

_____

- - - - - - - - - - - - - - - - - -

_____

_____

- - - - - - - - - - - - - - - - - -

_____

_____

- - - - - - - - - - - - - - - - - -

_____

Copyright © McGraw-Hill Education

Directions: Write the capital and lowercase forms of the letter *Cc* under each picture whose name begins with the /k/ sound.

Skills Practice 1 • Alphabetic Principle

Copyright © McGraw-Hill Education

B

Directions: Circle all pictures whose names end with the /b/ sound. Write the capital form of the letter *Bb* on the line.

Copyright © McGraw-Hill Education

b

Directions: Circle all pictures whose names end with the /b/ sound. Write the lowercase form of the letter *Bb* on the line.

1. Do you like bugs?
   Look at that bug!

2. Owen plays soccer.
   Owen scored a goal!

3. Penguins have feathers.
   I love penguins!

4. We are going to the zoo!
   How many animals are there?

5. I use glue in art class.
   Put those scissors down!

Directions: Listen carefully to each sentence I read. Circle the exclamation point.

Grammar, Usage, and Mechanics • *Skills Practice 1*

Copyright © McGraw-Hill Education

O o

O

o

Directions: Write the capital and lowercase forms of the letter Oo. Write the letter o under the picture whose name has the /o/ sound.

Copyright © McGraw-Hill Education

_____

- - - - - - - - - - - - - - - - - -

_____

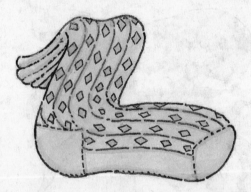

_____

- - - - - - - - - - - - - - - - - -

_____

Copyright © McGraw-Hill Education

Directions: Write the letter o under each picture whose name has the /o/ sound.

Penmanship • *Skills Practice 1*

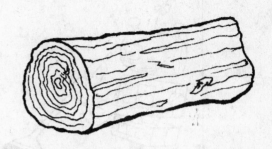

_____

- -

_____

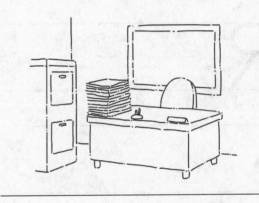

_____

- -

_____

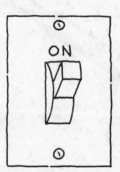

_____

- -

_____

Copyright © McGraw-Hill Education

Directions: Write the capital form of the letter O under each picture whose name begins with the /o/ sound. Write the lowercase form of the letter o under each picture whose name has the /o/ sound.

Skills Practice 1 • Alphabetic Principle

Rr

R -

r -

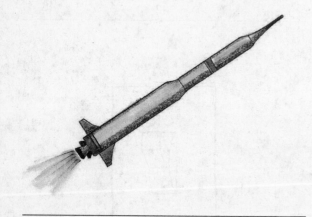

_____   _____

- - - - - - - - - - - - - - - -   - - - - - - - - - - - - - - - -

_____   _____

Copyright © McGraw-Hill Education

Directions: Write the capital and lowercase forms of the letter *Rr*.
Write the letter *r* under the picture whose name begins with the /r/ sound.

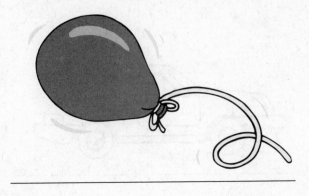

_____

- - - - - - - - - - - - - - -

_____

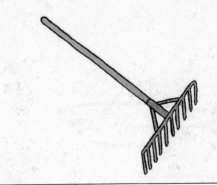

_____

- - - - - - - - - - - - - - -

_____

_____

- - - - - - - - - - - - - - -

_____

_____

- - - - - - - - - - - - - - -

_____

_____

- - - - - - - - - - - - - - -

_____

_____

- - - - - - - - - - - - - - -

_____

Copyright © McGraw-Hill Education

Directions: Write the letter *r* under each picture whose name begins with the /r/ sound.

_____   _____
- - - - - - - - - - - - - - - -   - - - - - - - - - - - - - - - -
_____   _____

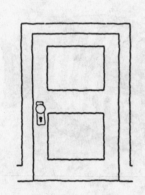

_____   _____
- - - - - - - - - - - - - - - -   - - - - - - - - - - - - - - - -
_____   _____

_____   _____
- - - - - - - - - - - - - - - -   - - - - - - - - - - - - - - - -
_____   _____

Directions: Write the capital and lowercase forms of the letter *Rr* under each picture whose name ends with the /r/ sound.

Copyright © McGraw-Hill Education

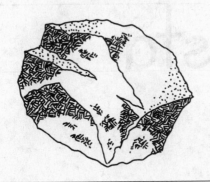

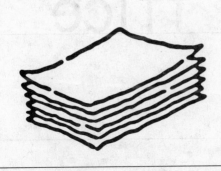

Directions: Listen carefully as I name each picture. Write the capital letter *R* under the pictures whose names begin with the /r/ sound. Write the lowercase letter *r* under the pictures whose names end with the /r/ sound. Write the letter *o* beside the other letter if you hear the /o/ sound.

Copyright © McGraw-Hill Education

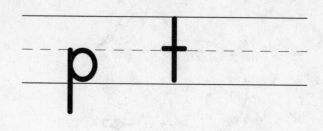

p t

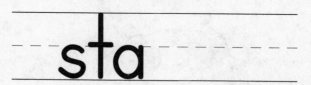

sta

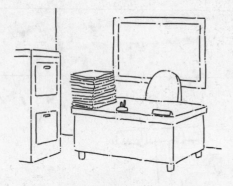

ffice

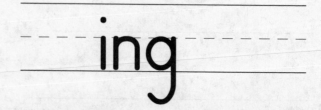

ing

Copyright © McGraw-Hill Education

Directions: Listen as I say each picture name. Write an *r* or an *o* to complete each word.

1. I see the white dog.
Do you see the dog?

2. Look at the horse.
Look at the horse with spots!

3. Mother read me a story.
Can you go to the bookstore?

4. He smells chicken soup.
Are they hungry for soup?

Copyright © McGraw-Hill Education

Directions: Listen carefully as I read each sentence and give the directions. Circle the correct answer.

Gg

G ----------------------------------

g ----------------------------------

Directions: Write the capital and lowercase forms of the letter *Gg*. Write the letter *g* under the picture whose name begins with the /g/ sound.

Copyright © McGraw-Hill Education

_____

- - - - - - - - - - - - - - - - - -

_____

_____

- - - - - - - - - - - - - - - - - -

_____

_____

- - - - - - - - - - - - - - - - - -

_____

_____

- - - - - - - - - - - - - - - - - -

_____

Copyright © McGraw-Hill Education

Directions: Write the letter *g* under each picture whose name begins with the /g/ sound.

pig   tag

_____

- - - - - - - - - - - - - - - - - - -

_____

rug   bug

_____

- - - - - - - - - - - - - - - - - - -

_____

pig   fig

_____

- - - - - - - - - - - - - - - - - - -

_____

bag   hug

_____

- - - - - - - - - - - - - - - - - - -

_____

Copyright © McGraw-Hill Education

Directions: Circle the word with the final /g/ sound that names the picture. Then write the letter on each line that makes the /g/ sound.

fog   log

_____

- - - - - - - - - - - - - -

_____

egg   leg

_____

- - - - - - - - - - - - - -

_____

hog   dog

_____

- - - - - - - - - - - - - -

_____

bag   wig

_____

- - - - - - - - - - - - - -

_____

Copyright © McGraw-Hill Education

Directions: Circle the word with the final /g/ sound that names the picture. Then write the letter on each line that makes the /g/ sound.

Skills Practice 1 • Alphabetic Principle

bat   hat

_____

- - - - - - - - - - - - -

_____

cat   tot

_____

- - - - - - - - - - - - -

_____

bug   dog

_____

- - - - - - - - - - - - -

_____

pot   drop

_____

- - - - - - - - - - - - -

_____

Directions: Circle the word that names the picture. Write the word you circled on the line.

Copyright © McGraw-Hill Education

Penmanship • *Skills Practice 1*

_____

- - - - - - - - - - - - - - - - - -

_____

_____

- - - - - - - - - - - - - - - - - -

_____

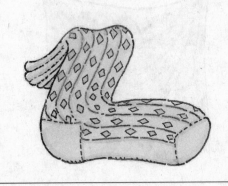

_____

- - - - - - - - - - - - - - - - - -

_____

_____

- - - - - - - - - - - - - - - - - -

_____

_____

- - - - - - - - - - - - - - - - - -

_____

_____

- - - - - - - - - - - - - - - - - -

_____

Copyright © McGraw-Hill Education

Directions: Write the letter *o* under each picture whose name has the /o/ sound. Find one picture name that begins with the /k/ sound and write *c* under it.

_____

- - - - - - - - - - - - - - - - - -

_____

_____

- - - - - - - - - - - - - - - - - -

_____

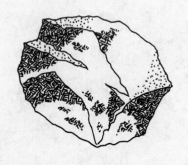

_____

- - - - - - - - - - - - - - - - - -

_____

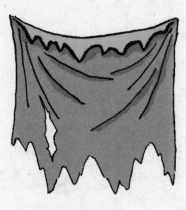

_____

- - - - - - - - - - - - - - - - - -

_____

_____

- - - - - - - - - - - - - - - - - -

_____

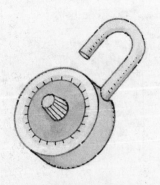

_____

- - - - - - - - - - - - - - - - - -

_____

Directions: Listen carefully as I name each picture. Write the letter o under each picture whose name has the /o/ sound. Write the letter r under the pictures whose names have the /r/ sound. Write the letter g under the picture if it has the /g/ sound.

Copyright © McGraw-Hill Education

1. I have a wagon.   T   A   S

2. Have you seen my shoes?   T   A   S

3. That is too heavy!   T   A   S

4. Have you seen that movie?   T   A   S

5. The apple tastes good.   T   A   S

6. Horses run fast.   T   A   S

Copyright © McGraw-Hill Education

Directions: Listen carefully as I read each sentence. Circle the letter *T* if the sentence tells something. Circle the letter *A* if the sentence asks something. Circle the letter *S* if the sentence shows strong feeling.

Jj

J

j

Directions: Write the capital and lowercase forms of the letter *Jj*. Write the letter *j* under the picture whose name begins with the /j/ sound.

Copyright © McGraw-Hill Education

_____   _____
- - - - - - - - - - - - -   - - - - - - - - - - - - -
_____   _____

Copyright © McGraw-Hill Education

_____   _____
- - - - - - - - - - - - -   - - - - - - - - - - - - -
_____   _____

Directions: Write the letter *j* under each picture whose name begins with the /j/ sound.

Skills Practice 1 • Alphabetic Principle

Name _____   **Date** _____

F F

F _

f _

_ _ _ _ _ _ _ _ _ _ _ _ _ _ _   _ _ _ _ _ _ _ _ _ _ _ _ _ _ _

Copyright © McGraw-Hill Education

Directions: Write the capital and lowercase forms of the letter *Ff*. Write the letter *f* under the picture whose name begins with the /f/ sound.

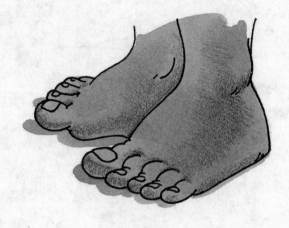

_____

Copyright © McGraw-Hill Education

Directions: Write the letter *f* under each picture whose name begins with the /f/ sound.

Skills Practice 1 • Penmanship

F –

Directions: Circle the objects in the pictures whose names begin with the /f/ sound. Write the capital form of the letter *Ff* on the line.

Copyright © McGraw-Hill Education

Copyright © McGraw-Hill Education

f —

Directions: Circle the pictures whose names end with the /f/ sound. Write the lowercase form of the letter *Ff* on the line.

fan   tan

_____

— — — — — — —

_____

pump   jump

_____

— — — — — — —

_____

hot   jam

_____

— — — — — — —

_____

fish   dish

_____

— — — — — — —

_____

Copyright © McGraw-Hill Education

Directions: Circle the word with the beginning /j/ or /f/ sound that names the picture. Then write the letter on each line that makes the /j/ or /f/ sound.

1. I see the dog.

   I see the dog's brown hair.
   The dog has brown hair.

2. Here is my lunch.

   I am eating a sandwich.
   Here is my sandwich.

3. He drew a picture.

   His picture is of a monkey.
   He drew a monkey.

Copyright © McGraw-Hill Education

Directions: Listen as I read the sentences. Circle the sentence below that has a different beginning.

Uu

U _____

u _____

____ - - - - - - - - - - - - - -   ____ - - - - - - - - - - - - - -

_____   _____

Copyright © McGraw-Hill Education

Directions: Write the capital and lowercase forms of the letter *Uu*. Write the letter *u* under the picture whose name has the /u/ sound.

_____   _____

- - - - - - - - - - - - - - -   - - - - - - - - - - - - - - -

_____   _____

Copyright © McGraw-Hill Education

_____   _____

- - - - - - - - - - - - - - -   - - - - - - - - - - - - - - -

_____   _____

Directions: Write the letter *u* under each picture whose name has the /u/ sound.

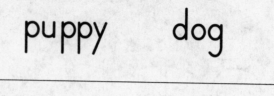
puppy   dog

_____

- - - - - - - - - - - - - - - -

_____

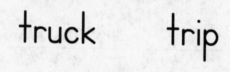
truck   trip

_____

- - - - - - - - - - - - - - - -

_____

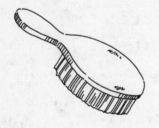

mesh   brush

_____

- - - - - - - - - - - - - - - -

_____

duck   quack

_____

- - - - - - - - - - - - - - - -

_____

Directions: Listen carefully as I say each word. Circle the word with the /u/ sound that names the picture. Then write the capital and lowercase forms of the letter *Uu* on each line.

Alphabetic Principle • *Skills Practice 1*

Copyright © McGraw-Hill Education

Name _____ **Date** _____

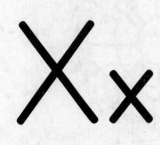

X

x

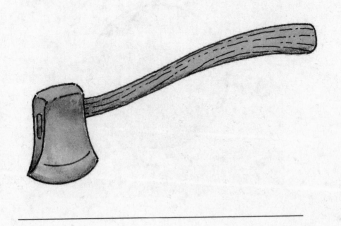

_____

- - - - - - - - - - - - - -

_____

_____

- - - - - - - - - - - - - -

_____

Copyright © McGraw-Hill Education

Directions: Write the capital and lowercase forms of the letter *Xx*. Write the letter *x* under the picture whose name ends with the /ks/ sound.

_____ _____

- - - - - - - - - - - - - - - - - - - - - - - - - - - -

_____ _____

_____ _____

- - - - - - - - - - - - - - - - - - - - - - - - - - - -

_____ _____

Copyright © McGraw-Hill Education

Directions: Write the letter x under each picture whose name ends with the /ks/ sound.

Alphabetic Principle • *Skills Practice 1*

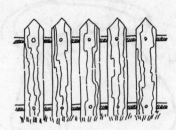

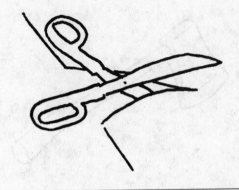

_____

- - - - - - - - - - - - - - - - - -

_____

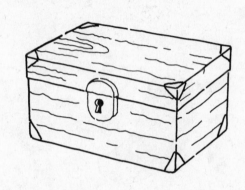

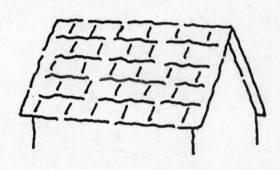

_____

- - - - - - - - - - - - - - - - - -

_____

_____

- - - - - - - - - - - - - - - - - -

_____

Copyright © McGraw-Hill Education

Directions: Write the capital and lowercase forms of the letter *Uu* under the pictures whose names have the /u/ sound.

Skills Practice 1 • Penmanship

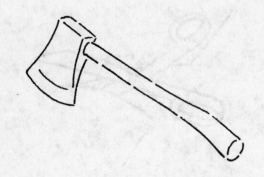

_____
- - - - - - - - - - - - - - - - - -
_____

_____
- - - - - - - - - - - - - - - - - -
_____

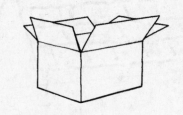

_____
- - - - - - - - - - - - - - - - - -
_____

_____
- - - - - - - - - - - - - - - - - -
_____

_____
- - - - - - - - - - - - - - - - - -
_____

_____
- - - - - - - - - - - - - - - - - -
_____

Directions: Write the capital and lowercase forms of the letter _Xx_ under the pictures whose names have the /ks/ sound.

Copyright © McGraw-Hill Education

1. Miss Molly makes a marbled   in the morning.

2. Floppy the fish flips his fins to get a  .

3. We wish we could watch the  wobble in the wind.

4. Can you carve a crib out of a clean ?

5. Nora needs a nickel, a new   , and a noodle in the night.

Copyright © McGraw-Hill Education

Directions: Listen carefully for sound patterns as I read each sentence. I will name each picture as I read.
Circle the picture that matches the sound pattern in the sentence.

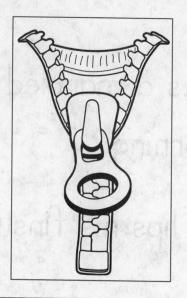

Z z

Z _____

z _____

_____

_____

Copyright © McGraw-Hill Education

Directions: Write the capital and lowercase forms of the letter Zz. Write the letter z under the picture whose name begins with the /z/ sound.

_____

- - - - - - - - - - - - - - -

_____

Copyright © McGraw-Hill Education

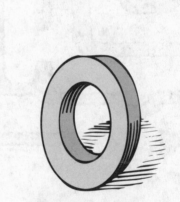

_____

- - - - - - - - - - - - - - -

_____

Directions: Write the letter z under each picture whose name begins with the /z/ sound.

rose

eggs

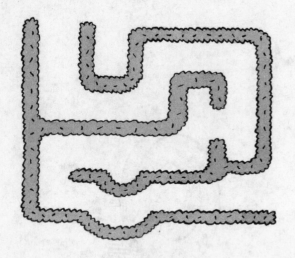

maze

buzz

Directions: Say each picture name. Circle the letter or letters in the name that make the /z/ sound.

Copyright © McGraw-Hill Education

prize

nose

fuzz

wigs

Copyright © McGraw-Hill Education

Directions: Say each picture name. Circle the letter or letters in the name that make the /z/ sound.

_____

- - - - - - - - - - - - - - - - - -

_____

_____

- - - - - - - - - - - - - - - - - -

_____

_____

- - - - - - - - - - - - - - - - - -

_____

Copyright © McGraw-Hill Education

Directions: Name each picture. Write the letter *j* if the name begins with the /j/ sound. Write the letter *f* if the name begins with the /f/ sound. Write the letter *u* if you hear the /u/ sound.

an

b g

ox

ar

Copyright © McGraw-Hill Education

Directions: Listen as I say the name for each picture. Write the missing letter on the line.

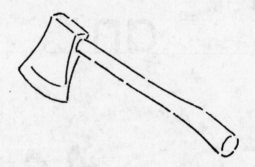

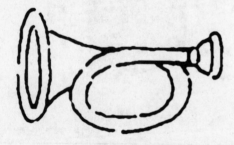

Copyright © McGraw-Hill Education

Directions: Listen as I say the name for each picture. Draw a line between the two pictures whose names have the /u/ sound. Draw a line between the two pictures whose names have the /ks/ sound. Draw a line between the two pictures whose names have the /z/ sound.

Alphabetic Principle • *Skills Practice 1*

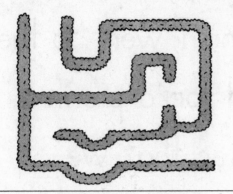

ma_e

m_g

_ork

_ebra

bo_

_acket

Directions: Listen as I say the name for each picture. Write the missing letter on the line.

Copyright © McGraw-Hill Education

One day, Marcus, Ray, and I went to the park.Marcus brought food for a picnic and we played games.After that we played on the playground.Later we took my dog for a walk around the park.All of us had a fun time.Suddenly a storm appeared in the sky.It had lightning and thunder.Marcus, Ray, and I ran home.

Directions: Listen carefully as I read the paragraph. Put a slash where a space should appear in the paragraph.

Copyright © McGraw-Hill Education